# SOCIAL HISTORY AND LITERATURE

NATIONAL BOOK LEAGUE SEVENTH ANNUAL LECTURE

# SOCIAL HISTORY
# AND LITERATURE

R. H. TAWNEY

LONDON

PUBLISHED FOR THE

NATIONAL BOOK LEAGUE

BY THE CAMBRIDGE UNIVERSITY PRESS

1950

# CAMBRIDGE
## UNIVERSITY PRESS

University Printing House, Cambridge CB2 8BS, United Kingdom

Cambridge University Press is part of the University of Cambridge.

It furthers the University's mission by disseminating knowledge in the pursuit of education, learning and research at the highest international levels of excellence.

www.cambridge.org
Information on this title: www.cambridge.org/9781107492271

First published 1950
Re-issued 2015

*A catalogue record for this publication is available from the British Library*

ISBN 978-1-107-49227-1 Paperback

# SOCIAL HISTORY AND LITERATURE

No one could follow without a sense of inadequacy the distinguished lecturers who have previously addressed you; nor is my diffidence diminished by reflection on the topic which I have been rash enough to select. Discourses introducing a particular discipline with prefatory commendations of the pleasures to be derived from it are apt to resemble those Chinese dramas the spectator of which, after listening for five hours to a succession of curtain-raisers, discovers that the performance is over at the moment when he hoped that it was about to begin. Some sage has remarked that foreign travel is supposed to broaden the mind, but too often, in reality, merely elongates the conversation. It would be regrettable if voyages through time, as well as through space, gave ground for that reproach; and discretion requires that a speaker, whatever the sufferings he may ultimately inflict, should, at least in his propitiatory opening, endeavour to avoid it. The motives which lead us to one or both of the allied interests mentioned in my title are obviously of great diversity; but some, and not the least cogent, have their source in the nature of man as a social being. To indicate the aims of the quest inspired by them, and the character of the rewards for which, when fortune smiles, it may hope, should not demand prolixity.

In a famous passage of the *Inferno* Ulysses speaks to Dante and Vergil of "the passion to win experience of the world and of human vice and worth", which drove him when, after his twenty years of wandering he had at length reached home, once more to set sail, on his last fatal

*

voyage. Whatever else the world may contain, man's relations with nature, his commerce with his fellows, and the convictions, aspirations and emotions composing his inner life, are for us, as for the poet, its capital constituents. No one can be fully at home either with it or with himself until, through the vicarious experience of which the vehicle is books, he has learned enough of the triumphs and tragedies of mankind to catch a glimpse of the heights to which human nature can rise and depths to which it can sink. To such comprehension, which less enlightened ages called wisdom, there is more than one road; but an acquaintance which, for most of us, only reading can convey with the methods by which men of like passions with ourselves have wrestled, in circumstances different from our own, with problems of individual and collective existence—religion, law and government, the conquest of the material environment and the ordering of social life—that are also ours, can make a modest contribution to it. It is part of the process by which we surmount the limitations of our isolated personalities and become partners in a universe of interests which we share with humanity. Not the least potent of the magicians who fling wide the windows opening on these vistas are the Muses who preside over History and Literature. Each rules a separate province, with laws of its own; but the debatable land where they inter-common is not small; and, like terrestrial states, their immaterial kingdoms flourish best when friendly intercourse between them is unimpeded by artificial barriers. Naturally, neither is without its riddles; and both offer ample opportunities for finished exhibitions of the great art of complicating the simple and obscuring the obvious by which the authentic intellectual proves his title to that proud name. I observe these gymnastics with admiration and awe; but a consciousness that the stratosphere is not my spiritual home deters me from imitating them. So, without attempting to add yet another to the philosophical rationalizations of activities which, if not as old as man, are in one form or another, coeval with his earliest written records, let me turn to my theme.

The humble branch of history, with which alone this evening I am concerned, cannot boast, like some of its more illustrious colleagues, that it supplies precedents and warnings of immediate utility in the conduct of great affairs. But the forces that figure most conspicuously before the footlights are not always those that set the stage; and, if studies dealing in the prose of common life neither breakfast with ministers nor dine at international conferences, they are not necessarily, for that reason, to be consigned to the limbo reserved for triviality. Each generation must write its history for itself, and draw its own deductions from that already written, not because the conclusions of its predecessors are untrue, but for a practical reason. Different answers are required, because different questions are asked. Standing at a new point on the road, it finds that fresh ranges of the landscape come into view, whose unfamiliar intricacies demand an amplification of traditional charts. It is obviously not an accident that when, after 1830, French thinkers reflected on the convulsions of the four preceding decades, the result should have been the search for the hidden cracks and fissures in the social order demolished by the earthquake, of which de Tocqueville's *L'Ancien Régime* remains a lofty landmark; or that England in the full tide of the Industrial Revolution should have provided Macaulay with the foil against which to throw into high relief, in his famous third chapter, the simpler society of an age politically brilliant, but, compared with his own, economically immature; or that the year of revolutions, in which his book appeared, should also have seen a less sanguine interpretation of

7

the material triumphs applauded by him begin, in the obscurity of a cheap pamphlet, a voyage that was to take it round the world; or that when, after 1870, the great industry and an urban civilization were in process of conversion from an insular peculiarity into European institutions, scholars of different nationalities and opposing views should have launched, with resources of knowledge and criticism not available to Marx, a debate on the historical origins of Capitalism which is not yet concluded. It was equally natural that a generation increasingly conscious of the problems posed by the profound changes in human relations which those movements had produced, should turn, with heightened curiosity, to works revealing the life of societies not yet affected by them or experiencing only their first disturbing impact.

Of the contributions of authors with widely varying interests—legal historians, writers whose interests were primarily economic, students of the development of local government and administration, experts on the history of particular localities, later geographers and ecologists—I must not pause to speak. By the end of the last century, not a few obscure departments of social life had been compelled to yield their secrets, and the doors into others since then unlocked have not been few. The adjective in my title is to be regarded, therefore, not as a signpost pointing to a recently discovered field, but merely as a reminder of riches already at our disposal, or waiting to be extracted from ground beneath our feet. All history has as its theme one aspect or another of collective life; and the function of Social History—if that term is to be employed—is not the enrolment of an additional recruit in the battalion of specialisms already at work. It is primarily, I suppose, to underline the truth that, if research requires a division of forces, a humane education requires a synthesis, however provisional, of the results of their labours, and to encourage us, by seeing those results, not as isolated fragments, but as connected parts of a body of living tissue, to acquire a more synoptic and realistic view of the activities composing the life of society. The subject, as I interpret it, is concerned not merely or mainly with the iridescent surface of manners, fashions, social conventions and intercourse, but with the unseen foundations, which, till they shift or crumble, most men in most generations are wont to take for granted. Nor, since human beings cannot live on air and rarely live alone, can public and private business—politics and economics—be excluded from its scope. These restless energumens are never so potent as when ignored; and notices to quit served on them in a preface rarely deter the pertinacious trespassers from slinking back into the text. The sensible course is to welcome them from the start as partners in a story which, the world being what it is, they have necessarily done much to shape.

Social history, thus conceived, can be approached by several paths. One, not the least pleasant and instructive, which starts from some familiar scene of daily life, I must not do more than mention. There are countries so unfortunate that a traveller can journey in them for several days with no companion but nature, who is delightful, but not, by herself, sufficient. England, like most of her European neighbours, is not among them. As in Mr. Chesterton's poem, it is "an island like a little book, full of a thousand tales". Something amusing or tragic has occurred at every corner; sweat, in the famous phrase, not to mention blood and tears, is thick on most of it. There are worse points of departure for history and those who teach it than the visible realities to which such associations cling. Some of them, I suppose, are treasured memories to most of us; and, of a hundred illustrations, one miniature must suffice. A tump—what the cultured call a *tumulus*—with neolithic

9

bones which the aged roadman at last consented not to throw away; a precipitate lane beside it, known to the natives, though not to writers of guide-books, as King Charles' Hill, because, on an early day in August, 1643, some enterprising staff officer contrived—Heaven knows how—to get the army down it on its way to the siege of the godly city the unforeseen tenacity of whose obstinate shopkeepers wrecked the year's campaign; twenty minutes one way the room in which, forty years before, the Catholic Throckmorton of the day had brooded with Catesby over projects for the famous plot; twenty minutes the other the farm called Abbey Farm, seized, two generations earlier, by the Defender of the Faith from a local religious house; a mile north the high point known as Wittentree Clump, where the wise men of the district are thought to have assembled in Saxon times and the Home Guard met in our own; a mile east a village not finally enclosed till the sixties of last century, in circumstances some of which—characteristically, the comic, not the sad—twenty years ago old men still recounted; a mile south the magnificent wrought-iron gates of the Haunted House, the work—so the probably mendacious story runs—of a smith convicted for murder, whom a wicked judge consented to spare, on condition that he made them, and then, when they were made, proceeded to hang; in the distance the hill from which, Mr. Madden [1] has told us, Clement Perks of the Hill, in *Henry IV*, took his designation, with the hamlet at its foot inhabited by the "arrant knave" favoured by Mr. Justice Shallow, the name of which is pronounced in the improbable manner in which Shakespeare, who, to judge by his spelling, must have heard it spoken, decided to write it—all, except the last, demand no more than tolerable boots and a longish afternoon. These human associations are as vital and moving a part of the landscape as its hills and streams. There are many districts, urban not less than rural, as rich or richer in them. If education does not use them, of what use are they? I have never taught children; so, like every one else in that position, I know exactly how to do it. A one-inch ordnance map as the teacher's bible; an attempt to lead the older of the little victims really to see and feel scenes every day beneath their eyes; a few good books, when such exist, in which to read of what they saw; and only then a gradual advance towards wider horizons—such would be some of the ingredients in my prescription.

All this, however, is a digression for which I apologize. Let me return to the more powerful ally invoked in my title, on whom all of us, wherever our lot is cast, can always lean. It seems to be of the nature of scholastic institutions, not least Universities, to proliferate to excess in the artificial entities known in the language of the trade as "subjects". When we reach years of discretion—which I take to mean the age when youth shows signs of getting over its education—part of our business is to join those naturally connected interests which the demands of examinations and the exigencies of time-tables have temporarily put asunder. The enjoyment of great literature is an end, not a means; and only a barbarian would degrade its timeless truths to the status of materials for a humbler art. But, to the charge of Philistinism, two pleas may be advanced.

Some familiarity, in the first place, with the scenes amid which the masters lived and worked—the disorderly, brilliant, vulgar, little London of the great age of the drama, vivid with the mingled gaiety and squalor of a street in Peiping; the ways of the polite society which idolized Pope; the East Anglian villages beneath whose tranquil surface Crabbe encountered his experiences "sad as reality and wild as dreams"; the fusion of the traditions of a border region still not wholly tamed with the influence of a city then not the least among the cultural capitals of Europe, which formed the mind of Scott—such knowledge not only is a tribute owed to genius by posterity, but can become, if kept in due subordination in the background of our minds, the foot of a ladder leading into the world of imagination which genius has created. It is equally true, in the second place, and more important for the historian, that literature opens windows on realities that would otherwise elude him. History, it is sometimes said, is concerned with facts; and, facts, Burns has remarked, in a line which I do not venture to quote, but which a friend has translated for me into gratuitously prosaic prose, do not shift their position, but remain unalterably what they are. There are, doubtless, many facts—though not, perhaps, so many as is sometimes supposed—which behave with the propriety ascribed to them by the poet. Some are more elusive monsters, of whom it may be said that to stay put, without entering into unanticipated and embarrassing combinations, is the last thing they can be trusted to do. Not a few are chameleons, which change their colour with the context in which they are seen and the eyes that see them.

To one poet who experienced it, the English Civil War was the vindication of providential justice; to a second, a reluctant soldier, a judgment on a people "by our lusts disordered into wars"; to a third, a "cause too good to have been fought for".[2] The mild and partial counter-revolution called the Restoration meant one thing to the writer of *Pilgrim's Progress*; another to the author of *Absalom and Achitophel*; a third to the Bishop—fat Tom Spratt—who composed the first history of the Royal Society; a fourth to the ex-cabin boy who, after rising to be Professor of Anatomy at Oxford and head of Cromwell's Army Medical Corps in Ireland, helped to found that famous body; showed his mettle by accepting a challenge to a duel, on condition that, since he was short-sighted, it should be fought in a dark cellar, with hatchets as the weapon;[3] and ended as not the least among the pioneers of English economic thought. A reader, if such a person exists, of the philosophical poem by Erasmus Darwin—the grandfather of the famous Charles—on the technological triumphs of his day, who turns from it to the work in which, just over a decade later, Southey described their seamy side, may be pardoned for failing to realize that the same people and period are depicted in both.[4] The first of the five years immediately preceding the second Reform Act saw the work by Ruskin on the social ethics of his fellow-countrymen, the publication of which in the *Cornhill Magazine* was discontinued by Thackeray, then its editor, on the ground that the moral sentiments of his sensitive readers were outraged by it; the third, the novel in which the immortal Mr. Podsnap announced the great truth that "this island is blessed, Sir, by Providence, to the direct exclusion of such other countries as there may happen to be"; the fifth, the classic in which the constitution of the chosen people was expounded by Bagehot, not without some hints, developed more at length in a later edition, that its best days might be over.[5]

The facts which elicited these diverse responses were obviously, in some sense, the same; but, not less obviously, they break into a hundred different facets. In order to understand the situations composed by clusters of them, it is necessary to undertake a voyage of circumnavigation, which enables the ambiguous mass to be seen and probed from different angles. Clever *litterateurs*, all glitter and fizz, are the worst company in which to make it; great authors are the best. Experiencing the agonies of the *mêlée*, but with the strength to stand above it, they grasp as a whole realities which those in the line see only in fragments, and often—battles being, in this respect, what they always

13                                             **

have been and always must be—do not see at all. More important, their vision is sharpened by an emotional receptiveness which lesser mortals lack. All branches of history present enigmas, which only labour can unravel. The sciolism which finds in infallible formulae of universal application a painless alternative to thought need not be considered, but even honest work is not without its snares. The analogy of some other sciences make it natural that some of those engaged in history should be pre-occupied, at times to excess, with questions of change, development and causation. That approach has its uses, but to view either an individual or a society primarily as a problem is to make certain of misconceiving them. Sympathy is a form of knowledge. It cannot be taught. It can only be absorbed by association with those the depth of whose natures has enabled them most profoundly to feel and most adequately to express it.

Generalities are unconvincing. Let me endeavour to illustrate these commonplaces by glancing for a moment at the society and literature of a period whose epic quality no later discoveries or re-interpretations are likely to impair. The duration to be assigned to the Elizabethan age varies with the aspect of its existence which is under consideration. It is not the same in international as in domestic politics. In literature it is longer than in either; and, as in the case of the Victorian era, the resemblance between the opening and concluding phases of the reign from which it takes its name are less marked than the contrasts. A mood, an attitude of mind, an outlook on life, can hardly be dated. If, however, a watershed is sought at which earlier doubts of the survival of the *régime* melt into the buoyant self-confidence of its middle years, the collapse, at the end of its first decade, of the last of the feudal and Catholic revolts may be regarded as marking it. It is at some point in the quarter of a century following that defeat of the old England by the new—the period when stability is assured and tempers, later to be spoiled by depression, the Irish fiasco and the war-taxation resulting from it, not yet set on edge—that the Elizabethan high noon may be said to begin. The phrase itself is of recent origin; but the sentiment expressed by it is not a modern idealization. Within a generation of the death of the Queen, the good days that ended with her were already a legend, to which antagonists soon to be at each others' throats continued to appeal at the moment when they were destroying the conditions that had produced it. The constitutional proprieties of the majestic past were to be invoked by Hyde; its sage, paternal authoritarianism by Wentworth; its anti-Spanish foreign policy, when that policy was out of date, by the house of Commons, and, later, by Cromwell; the success of its business diplomacy by the chief of the export kartels which spoke for the City; its conservative social reconstruction by the few who voiced the feelings of peasants and craftsmen; its indulgence to buccaneering and the non-commercial virtues by country gentlemen fretting for the golden days before, as one of them wrote, "peace and law had beggared us all".[6] The loftiest achievements of the literary movement fall outside the reign in which it began; but the 'eighties, with Sidney's *Apologie for Poetrie* and Marlowe's tragedies, are its magnificent youth; while the appearance in the same decade of Camden's *Britannia* and Hakluyt's *Voyages*, and, in the first year of the next, of the first three books of *The Faerie Queene*, reflects the mood of a generation conscious of having done some things worth remembering. When posterity speaks of the Elizabethan age, it is commonly, I suppose, that dazzling outburst of artistic genius that the words first recall.

Legends are apt to be fallacious in detail and true in substance. If the England of Elizabeth has a title to its reputation, the secret of its charm is not to be found in regions where a generation more refined might be disposed first to seek it. It is not humanity; for, judged by the standards of any period less debased than our own, its brutality was shocking. It flogged and branded the unhappy people whom poverty compelled to take the roads. In matters such as Catholic propaganda, where the safety of the state was thought to be at stake, it used torture without compunction. It practised, on occasion, a calculated atrocity in its treatment of the Irish. In England itself, the Northern rising had as its sequel, not only the punishment of great offenders, but an attempt to strike terror by mass executions of humble followers. Its long suit, again, was not enlightenment. It is needless to speak of its popular superstitions, sometimes innocent and graceful, sometimes barbarous; it is sufficient to recall that the view of the universe which appealed to many able and high-minded men as an improvement on them was that associated with the theology of Calvin. A forbearing and pacific spirit was not among its ornaments. Tempers were hasty; knives loose in the sheath. If, at home, private wars had ceased, private vendettas had not; while, abroad, the heroes of the maritime epic were justly denounced by their victims as pirates. Nor, finally, were saintliness and a reverence for it, which have redeemed some harsh ages, qualities much in esteem. A hard materialism, which saw the world in terms of title-deeds, rent-rolls and profits, was not a vice confined to worldlings. It had conspicuous devotees, not only, as would be expected, in business and at Court, but among the children of light on the episcopal bench.

If, therefore, a man has a taste for heavy shadows, he need not run short of paint. Yet, whatever the improprieties of the magician, his spell somehow works. When everything has been said—and much more might be said

—of the horrors of the time, there still floats over it all a turbid radiance, which, if difficult to seize and express, is not difficult to feel. The life of that quality is not long—two generations and it is almost dead—but, while it lasts, it is intoxicating. Everyone loves a lover, and it is partly what Arnold meant when, quoting Shakespeare's murderous Richard on the eve of the battle—"Stir with the lark tomorrow, gentle Norfolk"—he spoke of the note of the day as an inexhaustible gusto. It is the enthusiastic, high-spirited zest, enchanted with the world and not at odds with itself, which meets one, not only in the high places of poetry, but on the level plain of intimate letters and casual conversations, and which finds its way into literature because it is already in life. One hears it in one mood in the lament of one of Burleigh's correspondents on the men who fell in action: "Consider the thousands of brave English people that have been consumed by sea and land within these two years, [who] have not been rogues, cut-purses, horse-stealers, committers of burglary and other sorts of thieves (as some of our captains and men of war, to excuse themselves, do report) but in truth they were young gentlemen, yeomen and yeomen's sons, and artificers of the most brave sort, such as disdained to pilfer and steal, but went as voluntary to serve of a gaiety and joyalty of mind, all which kind of people are the flower and force of a kingdom".[7] One hears it in another in the innocent self-satisfaction, saved from arrogance by its artlessness, of Harrison's *Description of Britain*, where not only are "the artificers and husbandmen . . . so merry without malice and plain without inward Italian and French craft and subtlety that it would do a man good to be in company with them", but the cattle are larger and juicier than in less favoured lands; the mastiffs so humane that, when a parent is about to chastise his child, the generous creature snatches the rod from his hand; and the very mongrels—"whappets and prick-eared curs meet for many toys"—seem to wag their tails twice as fast as ordinary dogs.[8] One encounters it in a third guise in Nash's surprising rhapsody on the unexciting fish which made the fortune of East Anglian sea-ports—"the puissant red herring, the golden Hesperides red herring, the Maeonian red herring, the red herring of Red Herrings Hall, every pregnant peculiar of whose resplendent laud and honour to delineate and adumbrate to the ample life were a work that would drink dry four score and eighteen Castalian founts of eloquence, consume another Athens of facunditie, and abate the haughtiest poetical fury between this and the Zone and the Tropic of Cancer. . . . But no more will I spend on it than this: Saint Patrick for Ireland, Saint George for England, and the red herring for Yarmouth."[9] If, as has been said, the best sign of spiritual health is happiness, then I am unable to resist the conclusion that our benighted ancestors were not far from grace. Perhaps, in view of their crimes, they should have been; but, in these matters, the ways of Providence are notoriously past finding out.

To be charmed by this eager vivacity, sometimes innocent and naïf, often truculent, is not to succumb to the insipid and unplausible idyll of May-poles, merry peasants and benevolent squires. It is obvious that social geology is moulded largely by economic forces. It is obvious also that the composition and lie of the strata, and the weight of the pressure of the upper layers on the lower, reflect the thrusts and strains which such forces produce. It should be equally evident, however, that both the action of material interests and the fabric on which they work are not identical in all environments, but different in each, and that a particular combination of them may be either more or less favourable to social health. If, for a short time, Elizabethan England was in that respect fortunate, some reasons, at least, are not difficult to suggest. It was a loosely knit, decentralized society, whose pattern of existence was a round of individual activities in a framework fixed by custom. Throughout great areas, especially in the north and west from Cumberland to Devon, land resources abundant in relation to population produced both a moving agricultural frontier and a mentality and style of life which were semi-colonial. In these half-settled regions, the "wild wood" of the ballads, with its deer, its distinctive crafts, and its opportunities for lawless independence, was not only an economic ally, to whom their inhabitants looked for rough grazing, as well as timber and other forest products, but, in case of need, a trusted friend and refuge. The oft-told tale of *Adam Bell, Clym of the Clough, and William of Cloudeslee* spoke to them of adventures that might well be their own. The Forest of Dean—to give only one example—was an Alsatia into which, when popular feeling ran high, the Sheriff dared not venture. A peasant agitation under Charles, which, after starting in Dorsetshire, travelled *via* Wiltshire to the banks of the Severn, found in that untamed woodland the chance for a last stand.[10] The indignant Privy Councillor who remarked that his Majesty's Government seemed in a fair way to capitulate to a band of resurrected Robin Hoods, spoke more truly than he knew. Such conditions were, of course, the exception; but almost everywhere outside London, in agriculture, and, except for textiles, in most of the older crafts, the independent producers outnumbered the proletarian elements. Except among the nobility, and often among them, local sentiment was more powerful than class connections; personal relations than the play of the economic mechanism; custom than law; the wisdom of the elders and the lore of the region than stereotyped truths or fallacies standardized for mass consumption. The fact that, outside a few exceptional industries, most men worked for themselves, not for a master, did not make the Mouldys, Bull-Calfs, Feebles and the rest virtuous or even diligent; but it made them individuals, not ciphers. Tradition was a power; and tradition—of its nature, a social creation—set discordant claims and conflicting ambitions against a larger background of mutual comprehension.

On this little intimate world had come in the later sixteenth century an upward movement—the new horizons opened by discovery and, in spite of recurrent depressions, expanding trade; the stimulus to thought given by religious and political controversy; the sensation, as the bad days of the 'forties and 'fifties, with their orgy of aristocratic anarchy, receded into the past, that a corner had been turned, and better times begun. The life-long wage-earners, in most regions a minority, suffered seriously from rising prices; and mere *rentiers*, like some of the old-fashioned nobility, experienced a rough passage, until either they went under, as some of them did, or faced the new realities, rationalized their estate-management, and put their households on a business footing. The *bourgeois* elements in society, which formed the majority—peasants with enough land to produce a small surplus for the market; the more prosperous yeoman, small masters and tradesmen; the gentry who farmed their own lands or leased them to farmers; the business classes generally— had the wind behind them. As often, the immediate and remote results were not the same. The more distant consequence of it all was to impose on the traditional social fabric strains too severe for it to stand; but the first effect was different. It was to give a jolt to the established order strong enough to shake it out of its inertia, but not so violent as to shatter it. It was to arouse sleeping energies and stimulate them to intenser effort, without turning them loose, as two centuries later, to snatch and tear as they pleased.

The Elizabethan age has many different aspects. As a chapter of social history, it is best regarded, perhaps, as the child of that happy interlude between two worlds—between the meaningless ferocities of a feudalism turned senile, such as meet us a century earlier in *The Paston Letters*, and the demure austerities of the first, pious, phase of capitalism. Hence a gaiety and optimism, which were not merely superficial; a buoyancy as of youth, I will not say slightly intoxicated, but at any rate, in high spirits and at the top of its form. Its secret is energy working in an appreciative environment; an excellence—when there is excellence—not exclusive, but widely shared; a sense of individual achievement, which becomes something more than individual because it is sustained and invigorated by a strong community of sentiment.

Forces later to contend are for the moment in equilibrium. London and its nasty ways are a growing power; but they have not yet over-shadowed the provinces. National sentiment is strong; but local life goes its own way. Economic enterprise is expanding; but its requirements have not yet been erected into a final criterion of social expediency. Communal institutions—village, borough and guild—have suffered some rude shocks; but they are still active and vigorous. The Court is a magnet, though, compared with what it was to become, a feeble one; but the outburst of county histories and surveys, which began in the 1570's with Lambard's *Perambulation of Kent*, and which produced a score of similar works in the next half-century, reveals the pride of regional patriotism. Some of the newer industries, which were to dominate the future, are organized from the start on a capitalist basis, but they remain the exception. The character of the traditional productive system, with the few journeymen living, as in the works of Deloney and Dekker, as members of their master's family ; the wide distribution of property, which conferred on most men a certain dignity and status; the absence of caste barriers, which made trade a common interest; the fact that money counted more than birth, and for a time favoured new men by levelling old barriers; a common legacy of religious beliefs in which the Reformation, in England a political and social revolution rather than a spiritual upheaval, had made little change—all these influences had combined to produce an outlook on life which was surprisingly homogeneous. There is a converse fact, which is equally significant, but which I must not pause to develop. It is the enlarged opportunities open to forcible personalities, which make the tragedies of the time, not only on the stage, but in real life—consider, side by side with an Anthony and a Coriolanus, an Essex and a Raleigh—the destruction of greatness by the force of its own genius. The penalties on overweening ambition—"by this sin fell the angels"—are crushing; and, on the whole, it is felt to be right that such penalties should be imposed. Society is aristocratic; but most of its leaders stand too close to the public opinion of their districts to be the arrogant, egotistical oligarchy which later they became. In literature, painting and scholarship, the patron plays an important role; but culture is popular, in the sense that it draws on a body of experience which is not the monopoly of a single class, but is, in some degree, a general possession. It voices the outlook on life, not of an elegant *élite*, but of the world of common men.

The last point is often obscured by our habit of departmentalizing history, but it is not without significance. If any one doubts the connection between the quality of intellectual activities and the dull facts of social systems, let him consider both in two periods which one long lifetime sufficed to span. Few ages have so clearly revealed their soul in their art as that which began with the Restoration and reached its zenith a century later. One may be captivated by that art, or repelled by it, or feel, in different moods, each sentiment in turn; but neither admirers nor critics are likely to deny that the excellence of its greatest specimens reflects, and consciously reflects, the tone of a society whose rulers are divided by a chasm from the common herd. By the end of the first decade of the eighteenth century, native music is almost extinct; Handel, who first visited London in 1706, and Italian opera, rule alone. The domestic architecture of the well-to-do is sometimes distinguished, sometimes heavily pretentious; but whether majestic, or a mere monument of frigid ostentation, it bears its meaning on its face. Its aim is to be cosmopolitan, classical, less the enlargement of a native style than a repudiation of it. The drama, though not dead, is sick—sick of a resolute determination to be, before all things, genteel, with classical or foreign models to maintain an elevated tone, and smoking-room guffaws or drawing-room witticisms in place of humour. The prose is often admirable, but it also has changed; not imagination or eloquence, but lucidity, urbanity, decorum, are its characteristic virtues. The poetry is a well-managed instrument; at its best, a splendid exercise in the grand manner. Even the trifles tell the same story. As archaeologists know, there are worse clues to the convictions of a period than the tombs prepared by it for its dead. The characteristic feature of the sepulchral monuments of the Augustan age is not merely the chubby cherubim, too fat to fly, squatting heavily on some of them; it is the note struck in the epitaphs. Dreadful memories of fierce fanaticisms have caused "moderation" to be the chief virtue selected for commendations; "enthusiasm" has become the damning vice. The momentous discovery has been made that the words "truly respectable" are a reliable passport to Heaven.

Whatever the crimes of the Elizabethans, respectability

23

was not among them. From the Imperial Votaress, who was at home enough in the classics to chastise the indiscretions of a foreign ambassador in *ex tempore* Latin, but who also, when annoyed, swore in the vernacular like a fishwife, described the House of Commons as an assembly of devils, and boxed noble ears, to the drama, with the violence, buffoonery and hearty coarseness which have caused a foreign critic to denounce it as a riot of savages, and from the drama to everyday life, the note of it all was a genial, passionate vulgarity. The contempt, outside small circles, for the severer economic virtues—he "lives like a hog" was a criticism passed, not on poverty-stricken squalor, but on the sordid parsimony of a noble miser—the emphasis on lavish expenditure, rather than income, as the mark of social status; the indiscriminate profusion of the great households; the readiness of peasants with a grievance to fly to arms; the horseplay of London apprentices mobbing an unpopular foreign dignitary with the cheerful indifference to the proprieties of a body of Chinese students, are all, in their different ways, examples of it. Nothing is common or unclean. Different sides of life are not kept in closed compartments, but fertilize each other. Eminent men are eminent in half-a-dozen different ways at once; among those who are not, work, amusement, religion, adventure and a little fighting, are all stirred in one bowl. Descriptions of Shakespeare as a lawyer, schoolmaster, soldier and sailor, as well as a poet and actor-manager, are not, it seems, according to light; but such versatility, had he shown it, would have been quite in the Elizabethan manner. Stubbe's *Anatomy of Abuses*, or half a century later, Prynne's appalling pamphlet in seven hundred folio pages, suggest that it was this intemperate catholicity, even more than graver lapses, which smelled to Puritans of Hell-fire, as it was Puritan fastidiousness, walking like a cat on ice, and talking sanctified commonplaces through its elevated nose, which made it hateful to the Sir Toby Belches, who had no objection to virtue in moderation, but liked cakes and ale as well. In the literature of the time there is plenty of all three. It takes its materials where it finds them, in Plutarch or Cheapside, in Gloucestershire or Montaigne; has friends at the cheerful address later invented by Bunyan, an Elizabethan converted and conscious of sin—"Flesh Lane, over against the Church, hard by *The Sign of the Conscience seared with a Hot Iron*"— reeks heavily of the soil, and is not ashamed of its origins.

That is so in the case of the art then most widely loved and practised. Miss Jones, in her admirable work on the Charity Schools of the eighteenth century, recounts that those of England, though not of Wales, excluded from their curricula singing and ballads—"profane and loose poems set to music"—as calculated both to corrupt the morals of the young, by encouraging them "to put too great value upon themselves", and to undermine "the grand law of subordination" on which society reposed.[11] Elizabethan authoritarianism had its seamy sides; but, if its hands were often rough, its nerves were good. Once firmly in the saddle, it was not frightened of its fellow-countrymen, and these refinements of precautionary zeal —today only too familiar—were foreign to its simple mind. One of the first characteristics, indeed, of English life to strike observers was the diffusion among all classes of a passion for music. The styles of composers were not, it seems, unaffected by it. "The new wave of musical activity in singing and playing in the second half of the sixteenth century", writes a recent historian, "proves most eloquently that the ordinary folk, especially the peasantry, were not only not incapable of creative thought, but a very important part of Elizabethan musical life. In turn, the art of the higher regions of society was most strongly influenced by the vigour in the cultural activities of the common people in their popular pageants, folk songs and dances. ... The popular element was still prominently displayed in early Jacobean chamber music."[12]  It need not be assumed that works of individual genius—the madrigals and part-songs of Morley or the solo-songs of Danyell and Doweland—were consciously coloured, though they may have been, by folk-melodies. The significant fact is the existence of a public whose spontaneous appetite for musical enjoyment made it alert to welcome and transmit them. Somewhat the same might be said of the craft, whose range, next to agriculture, was the most extensive. The best of our local historians, Dr. Hoskins of Leicester, has expressed the view that, in the eighty years between the accession of Elizabeth and the meeting of the Long Parliament, the greater part of rural England was rebuilt. The English climate is not kind to wooden buildings, and some of the finest seventeenth-century specimens of the art are to be seen, far from the country which created it, in the woodlands of New England; but there are regions, like the limestone belt, of durable structures where the truth of his statement is visible to the eye. Since, apart from occasional depressions, agriculture and textiles were doing well, everyone was building; and everyone had the same necessities to meet; the same rain to carry off; except for such natural differences as those which existed between the stone, wood and clay districts, the same materials to use; and, within those large divisions, much the same idea as to what a house should be like. Hence, apart from variations in size, which are, of course, striking, the style of most of the domestic buildings of the period—the smaller manor-houses and farms, the barns and cottages—tends, in a given locality, to be all of a piece. Like their owners, the two former have been up and down in the world a score of times. Only one who knows their individual histories can tell them apart.

26

In literature, since it is less directly a response to natural needs, the complexities are greater; but, here again, similar influences were at work. The proper starting-point, in considering them, is the character of common speech. When an Elizabethan spoke of "my country", he commonly meant, not "my nation", but what a Frenchman means by *"mon pays"*—my province, district or county. There are some grounds for thinking, though certainty is impossible, that most members of most classes, not excluding many of the gentry, talked dialect at home; but the terms employed are less significant than the attitude revealed in the manner of using them. Consider two quotations: "As sheep or lambs are a prey to the wolf or lion, so are the poor men to the rich men "; "Wicked people, in conditions more like to wolves or cormorants than to natural men, that do most covetously seek to hold up the late great prices to corn and all other victual by engrossing the same into their private hands . . .; against which foul, corrupt fraud and malicious greediness there are both many good laws and sundry orders of late years given" . . . The vivid, concrete words, the anger expressed in a simple, hard-hitting phrase, are the same in both. But the first was a remark made by one of the Norfolk peasants who rose with Ket in the agrarian revolt that, seventy years later, was still recalled, as an awful warning, by speakers in the House during the debate on the first abortive general Enclosure Bill, and who was probably hanged in the course of the next fortnight; the second is part of an order on the subject of price-controls addressed by her Majesty's Privy Council to the Justices of Norfolk.[13] It is as though today a statement by the Ministry of Food were expressed with the violent directness of the language to be heard in queues, and the language of queues possessed the formal solemnity of Whitehall English, without its circumlocutions. That common quality of speech was not a mere trifle. Men spoke as they felt, and they felt as they lived. Since all, or nearly all, of them lived, as the Litany once a week reminded them, in intimate dependence on a capricious and tyrannical nature, their feelings on most subjects were much the same. Much is said and justly, of the ferocity of their religious conflicts. It is equally significant, though less often remembered, that those conflicts themselves could not have occurred but for the common premise supplied by a general agreement as to the transcendent importance of the ground of dispute.

Like all great literatures, that of Elizabethan England drank from many springs, foreign as well as native; but a community of understanding, which did not preclude sharp collisions of economic interest, was the soil in which it grew. Life, for all classes, was more spectacular, and, in a sense, more ceremonious, than it is today. Popular culture, before the Bible became a household book, was predominantly an oral and visual culture. Ballads, such as that which, when recited by a blind crowder, stirred the blood of Sidney; sermons; an occasional play; and social activities born of the daily intercourse of neighbours, were the food which fed it. The Bible itself, when added to them, offered incitements to almost too dramatic action. The imagination of common men worked at times with a spontaneous intensity which an epoch that has starved it finds difficult to grasp. The methods—one might almost say the ritual—of peasant risings, offer one example of its power. The mysterious leader—a Jack of the style, a Piers Plowman, a Captain Pouch "sent of God to satisfie all degrees whatsoever", a Lady Skimmington—in the infancy of Elizabeth, the banner with a plough, and the four captains of Penrith, Faith, Pity, Poverty and Charity, who march with drawn swords round Burgh church; in the later years of her successor, the play composed by a village schoolmaster for the commoners of Kendal, in which landlords are shown as ravens tearing in hell the entrails of sheep, their tenants—such episodes reveal popular emotion creating naturally and swiftly, at moments of excitement, a symbolism to express it.[14] Some of the later proceedings, indeed, of the Diggers, who inherited that tradition, and whose name meets us in the Midlands half a century before Winstanley made it for a moment a word of fear, are best regarded, not merely as pedestrian essays in practical land reform, but as half-symbolical acts, bringing light to a people sitting in darkness by an ocular manifestation of the New Law of Righteousness.

The imaginative vivacity which, when fired by a crisis, produced the poetry of action, flowed, in the tranquil routine of normal life, though different channels, but was sustained and invigorated, not stifled, by it. In villages, a round of recurrent activities—May-games; Whitsun, Easter and Christmas festivities; Church-ales; yearly wakes; occasional "gatherings for Robin Hood", such as, on one occasion, had deprived an indignant Latimer of his congregation; days off under Lords of Misrule, elected by "all the wildheads of the parish", with followers in "liveries of green, yellow or some light wanton colour; . . . about either leg twenty or forty bells", and "hobby-horses, dragons and other antics"; now and then a performance got up by Snug the joiner and Flute the bellows-mender, like that of which Shakespeare makes affectionate fun—in the larger villages called towns, gild pageants and plays, and sometimes, as at Gloucester, a "mayor's play", which, as one who saw it as a child wrote long after, "took such an impression on me that, when I came to man's estate, it was as fresh in my mind as if I had seen it newly acted"— these and similar diversions, if not universal, appear to have been widespread.[15] Thus the taste for seeing life dramatized was not a novelty, but a long-established habit, which formed, like the seasonal tasks of the agricultural year, an inseparable part of the traditional stuff of every-day existence. The Elizabethan, like the Athenian, drama, was an eminently social thing. Such humble enjoyments added their mites to the miracles created by it. Its greatest period was short, and passed through several phases. In the first, from the 1580's to the early years of James, popular tastes appear to have predominated in the public theatre, and popular and courtly entertainments to have influenced each other. It is not surprising that the picture of Shakespeare's audience drawn by Mr. Bennett, or, for that matter, by Ben Jonson—"capricious gallants", "the rankest stinkard", "the rude barbarous crew", "a fellow that comes . . . once in five years, at a parliament time", interspersed with a majority "very acceptive and apt to applaud any meritable work"—should remind us, in miniature, of the crowd at a cup-tie final.[16]

The Elizabethan spirit did not die with Elizabeth. The greatest of its literary achievements belong to the first half of the next reign; and it survives, an intermittent voice, down to and beyond the political breakdown. One hears the authentic note in that charming poem, composed by—of all people—a bishop,[17] "Farewell Rewards and Fairies". One encounters it in another key, when, in turning over the business papers of a City magnate on the road to high political office, one discovers, scrawled by him on the back of a dull account,[18] the lines ascribed to Raleigh on the night before his execution,

> E'en such is time, that takes on trust
> Our youth, our joys, our all we have,
> And pays us but with earth and dust. . . .

and realizes that there were moments when, for all his sanguine self-assurance, the conqueror was visited amid his triumphs by thoughts of the kind later immortalized in Shirley's justly famous song. It meets us, in different guises, in that delightful book, half biography, half the historical ramblings of the humanest of antiquaries, John Smith's *Lives of the Berkeleys*; or in Fuller's *Holy and Profane State* and *The Worthies of England*; or in passages of Sir Thomas Browne; or later, a belated echo, in Walton's *The Compleat Angler*, which, though not always infallible—unless the capricious creatures have changed—on the ways of trout, is admirable on human beings. But the balanced society of the great age—economic interests encouraged, but kept in their place; authority masterful, but popular sentiment a power—did not last. There were contemporaries who realized, when the new century was still young, that something had gone wrong.

The influence of the Court, the hypertrophy of the metropolis, the portentous inflation of the legal profession, the supposed wickedness of Roman Catholics, the alleged hypocrisy of Puritans, the advance of the money-power, were all put in the dock. The favourite target of the dramatists was the last. The greatest of all—

> Is not he just which all things doth behold
> From highest Heaven, and bears an equal eye?

—makes his own universe; but few, save he, are an exception to the statement. On the economic background of it all, I must not dwell. It is sufficient to say that, with the Anglo-Spanish Treaty of 1604, which wound up twenty years of conflict, followed two years later by a Treaty of Commerce between England and France, and later again by the twelve years' truce between Spain and the Netherlands, Europe, though not without wars and rumours of wars on her Eastern marches, slid half-unconsciously into one of her brief lucid intervals. The long commercial boom, which in England was one of the results of that partial pacification, not only meant a sensational expansion of international trade, but combined with the effects of continued inflation and the opportunities offered by the financial necessities of the Government to produce a series of speculative orgies on the London market, and a rash of new fortunes. Dekker, whose charming picture of craft life in *The Shoemaker's Holiday* is known to everyone, expresses the popular view of the *parvenu* plutocracy and its values in the picture of the merchant, Barterville, with his creed that

> Nature sent man into the world alone,
> Without all company, to serve but one,
> And that I'll do,

and the comment on that remorseless individualism passed by his attendant devil: "True City doctrine, Sir".[19] The verdict of a writer of loftier stature and far wider range was not very different. There is, of course, much else in Ben Jonson; but, as Professor Knights[20] has suggested, some of his most admirable plays, with their company-promoters, land-grabbers and monopolists, are partly the criticism of a traditional code of social ethics on old vices on the way to be sanctified as new virtues. Middleton, who produced in *The Changeling* a play described by some as the greatest tragedy of the period outside Shakespeare, reveals in his comedies of London life a different aspect of the same transformation. Massinger's Sir Giles Over-reach, a satire on the notorious Mompesson, and his outrageous Lady Frugal, are studies, if diluted ones, on Jonsonian themes. All of these writers were too good artists to turn their plays into sermons. None of them, in observing the world about him, could fail to seize and express the erosion of accepted standards of social conduct, which was among its most conspicuous features.[21]

The situation which evoked such responses from the dramatists could be illustrated in a score of different ways, from rural lamentations at the supersession by sharp business men of the easy-going ways of the old-fashioned landlord, or the struggle of London craftsmen against capitalist encroachments, or the more general exasperation aroused by the multiplication of parasitic interests based on concessions wrung from royal favour, to the elaboration of the metropolitan money-market by the practitioners whom an economically half-sophisticated age denounced, while it courted them, as damnable usurers. It was accompanied by a second change, of equal significance. Dryden, in speaking of the vogue enjoyed at the Restoration by Beaumont and Fletcher, remarks of the latter that he "understood and imitated the conversation of gentlemen much better" than Shakespeare.[22] In view of the volume and variety of their work, much of which, if it rarely scales the heights, is pleasing, it would be less than just to say that they understood nothing else; but it is difficult not to feel, in reading them, that Dryden's praise has more than one edge. It is true that, by their time, the public for which plays are composed is ceasing to be the noisy, passionate crowd of the past, in which educated and illiterate, fastidious connoisseurs and lovers of horseplay and blood, had jostled each other. It is true that they are the dramatists, less of Shakespeare's hydra-headed multitude, than of polite society. With them, and still more with Shirley and Brome, the later Comedy of Manners, which turns on the contrast between "the good form" of the fashionable world and the "bad form" of everyone outside it, is already on the way.[23] By, in fact, the accession of Charles, the days of comprehensiveness and profusion— the days of which it may be said, as Dryden said of Chaucer, "Here is God's plenty", are drawing to a close. Interests formerly united fall apart. High spirits and a good conscience are less often than in the past at ease with each other. Imagination and reason begin to go their separate ways. Virtue becomes self-conscious. Poetry, some of it

33

admirable, is more at home at court than in the tavern. The natural activities and amusements of men are a problem for moralists. Mercy and Truth, if they meet together, too often meet only to part. Righteousness is not deeply in love with Peace, and, in her austerer moments, strongly disapproves of kissing. Less than twenty years, and she is cutting Peace's throat.

The interplay between the practical activities of a society and the imponderables of emotion, moral sentiment and taste revealed in its art is not, of course, a feature peculiar to a single age. A reader who turns from the brief chapter in the life of a minute population—less than half that of greater London—to which this evening I have confined myself, to the two volumes of *Johnson's England*, edited by the late Professor A. S. Turberville, or to the works of Mr. G. M. Young on its Victorian successor, will find on more crowded, and to many more attractive, canvases abundant illustrations of the same theme. The significance of such affinities, it need hardly be said, is misconceived, when they are used as a basis for *naïvetés*, such as economic interpretations of culture. The day when these extravagances—half platitude, half fallacy—could be excused by the neglect of the factor emphasized by them is now long over. The oft-quoted words of Hamlet on the limitations of science, which he and his age meant by the word "philosophy", and which continued to be so designated for another two centuries,[24] supply the proper comment on them. The truth is that, apart from a few commonplaces, we know at present next to nothing of the relations, if such exist, between the artistic achievements of an epoch and the character of its economic life, and that the only candid course is to confess our ignorance. The attitude which best becomes us is a more modest one than the psycho-analytic ingenuity which discovers in great writers influences that they neither express nor would have understood. It is not to explain—whatever in such a connection that ambiguous word may mean—the efflorescence of genius. It is to rejoice in, admire and reverence its works. It is because the reading of History in conjunction with Literature may foster that attitude, that I have ventured to speak of them together.

# NOTES

The following notes and references to books have been contributed by Dr. Tawney:

[1] D. H. Madden, *The Diary of Master William Silence* (Longmans, Green, 1907, pp. 8, 3–7, 380–3). Madden's identification of "the hill" with Stinchcombe appears to be accepted by Professor Herford. See *The Works of Shakespeare* (Editor, C. H. Herford, Eversley Edition: Macmillan, 1899–1900, 10 vols. Vol. VI, p. 494 *note*). Woncot (Woodmancote) is now part of Dursley.

[2] John Milton, *The Tenure of Kings and Magistrates*, 1649 (Editor, W. T. Allison, New York, 1911), and *A Defence of the People of England*, 1650, see (John Milton, *Prose Works*, various publishers); Henry Vaughan, *The Constellation*, see *The Works of Henry Vaughan* (Editor, A. B. Grosart, Fuller Worthies' Library, 1870–1, 4 vols. Vol. I, p. 157), and *Ad Posteros*, see (*ibid.*, Vol. II, pp. 172–3), and for Vaughan's military service: F. E. Hutchinson, *Henry Vaughan: a Life and Interpretation* (Oxford University Press, 1947, chap. V). The words of Andrew Marvell occur in one of his less exhilarating works, *The Rehearsal Transposed*, see *The Complete Works in Verse and Prose of Andrew Marvell* (Editor, A. B. Grosart, Fuller Worthies' Library, 1872–5, 4 vols. Vol. III, p. 212).

[3] Sir William Petty's acceptance of the challenge is recounted by Evelyn, see *Diary and Correspondence of John Evelyn* (Editor, William Bray, Colburn, 1850–52, 4 vols. Vol. II, p. 96; Vol. III, p. 392).

[4] Erasmus Darwin, *The Botanic Garden: a Poem in two Parts*. Part I, *The Economy of Vegetation*; Part II, *The Loves of the Plants, with philosophical notes* (London, 1794–5, 2 vols.); Robert Southey, *Letters from England* (London, 1807, 3 vols. Vol. I, pp. 303–8; Vol. II, pp. 139–53; Vol. III, pp. 132–4.)

[5] John Ruskin, *Unto this Last: Four Essays on the First Principles of Political Economy* (Smith Elder, *now* Murray, 1862), and J. A. Hobson, *John Ruskin, Social Reformer* (Nisbet, 1898, p. 42); Charles Dickens, *Our Mutual Friend*, 1864–5 (various publishers), and William Bagehot, *The English Constitution*, 1867 (various publishers).

[6] John Oglander, *A Royalist's Note-book. The Commonplace Book of Sir John Oglander of Nunwell.* (Transcribed and edited by Francis Bamford, Constable, 1936, p. 14.)

[7] Historical Manuscripts Commission, *MSS. of the Marquis of Salisbury* (Part IV, pp. 4–5).

[8] William Harrison, *An Historicall description of the Islande of Britayne*, *etc.*, in Raphael Holinshed, *The firste Volume of the Chronicles of England*, 1577, 1587, etc. (See Book II, chap. VI; Book III, chap. I; Book III, chap. VII of 1587 edition.) A more handy work to use is *Elizabethan England, from a "Description of England" by William Harrison* (W. Scott, 1889), edited by Lothrop Withington, with an introduction by F. J. Furnivall, which contains selections from Harrison: see especially pp. 94–5, 151–2, 184.

[9] Thomas Nashe, *Lenten Stuffe*, see *The Complete Works of Thomas Nashe* (Editor, A. B. Grosart, Huth Library, 1881–5, 6 vols. Vol. V, pp. 307–8).

[10] S. P. D., Chas. I, CXCIV, 60, I–V; CXCV, 5; CCIII, 7, 36 and 57; CCXV, 57; CCXVI, 42 and 77: P. C. R., 1631, April 5 and 8, June 22, July 16, August 31; 1632, April 4 and 20.

[11] Mary Gwladys Jones, *The Charity School Movement: a Study of Eighteenth Century Puritanism in action* (Cambridge University Press, 1938).

[12] Ernest H. Meyer, *Elizabethan Chamber Music: the history of a great art from the Middle Ages to Purcell* (Lawrence & Wishart, 1946).

[13] For the quotations, see *Original Papers of the Norfolk and Norwich Archaeological Society* (1905, p. 22), and *Stiffkey Papers* (Camden Society, Third Series, Vol. XXVI, 1915, p. 140); for the text of the enclosure bill of 1621, W. Notestein, F. H. Relf and H. Simpson, *Commons Debates, 1621*, Yale University Press, New Haven, 1935, 7 vols. Vol. VII, pp. 112–19; and for references by speakers to the revolt of 1549, *ibid.*, III, pp. 186–7, and V. pp. 148–9.

[14] For the first three leaders, see R. H. Tawney, *The Agrarian Problem in the Sixteenth Century* (Longmans, Green, 1912, pp. 318, 333–4); for Lady Skimmington, S. P. D., Chas. I, CXCIII, 66; CXCIV, 60, I–V; CCIII, 36; for the banner with a plough and four captains of Penrith, Tawney, *op. cit.*, pp. 318–19; for the play performed at Kendal in 1621, Mildred Campbell, *The English Yeomen under Elizabeth and the Early Stuarts* (Yale University Press, New Haven, 1942: Yale Historical Studies, Vol. XIV, pp. 150–3). Its occasion was a struggle over tenant-right in the barony of Kendal. The issue came before the Court of Star-Chamber, and was decided in favour of the tenants.

[15] For May festivities, church-ales, wakes and lords of misrule, see Philip Stubbes, *Anatomy of Abuses in England*, 1583 (Editor, F. J. Furnivall, New Shakespeare Society, 1877, pp. 146–54); for gatherings for Robin Hood, Hugh Latimer (Bishop of Worcester), *Sermon preached before Edward VI*, 12 April, 1549, see *Seven Sermons preached before Edward VI* (Arber English Reprints, 1895), also *Sermons* (Everyman's Library: Dent); for the Mayor's play at Gloucester, R. Willis, *Mount Tabor: or Private Exercises of a Penitent Sinner*, 1639. As Willis was born in 1564, the morality play which so much impressed him *The*

*Cradle of Security*, in which three ladies represented pride, covetousness and luxury; the prince, wickedness and two old men, the end of the world and the last judgment, was presumably performed at Gloucester some time in the 1570's. Useful selections from the above and other contemporary works will be found in *Life in Shakespeare's England* by J. Dover Wilson (Cambridge University Press, 1911; Penguin Books, 1944).

[16] H. S. Bennett, *Shakespeare's Audience*, Annual Shakespeare Lecture of the British Academy (Oxford University Press, 1944, see *Proc. Brit. Ac.*, Vol. XXX); Ben Jonson, *The Case is Altered*, Act II, Scene iv, see *Works* (Editors, C. H. Herford and Percy Simpson, Oxford University Press, Vol. III, 1927).

[17] Richard Corbet, 1582–1634, Bishop of Oxford and Norwich, *A Proper New Ballad intituled The Fairies Farewell or God-a-mercy Will*; "to be sung or whistled to the tune of the Meadow Brow by the learned; by the unlearned to the tune of Fortune ". See *The Poems of Richard Corbet* (edited with biographical notes and a life of the author by Octavius Gilchrist, Longmans 1807). This is the fourth edition, with considerable additions. *The Fairies Farewell* is also reprinted in *A Treasury of Seventeenth Century English Verse, 1616–1660* (Editor, H. J. Massingham, Macmillan, 1919). Another edition is decorated by C. Lovat Fraser and privately printed, London, 1916.

[18] *Cranfield MSS.* 6118. The account is contained in a letter to Cranfield from one Richard Blackall, and gives particulars of customs duties received on Spanish or sweet wines, in which Cranfield was financially interested. Blackall's letter is dated from Exeter, 18 Oct. 1618, and presumably reached Cranfield in the course of the next week or ten days. Raleigh was executed on 29 Oct. 1618. Cranfield's version of Raleigh's lines differs slightly from that commonly printed today.

[19] Thomas Dekker, *If it be not good, the Devil's in it*, 1612, see *Dramatic Works* (Editor, R. H. Shepherd, J. Pearson, 1873, 4 vols. Vol. III, p. 322).

[20] L. C. Knights, *Drama and Society in the Age of Jonson* (Chatto & Windus 1937). I should like to acknowledge my indebtedness to Professor Knights for ideas and illustrations.

[21] The following plays may, in particular, be mentioned in this connection: Ben Jonson, *Volpone, The Alchemist, The Devil is an Ass*, see *Works* (Editor, C. H. Herford and Percy Simpson, Oxford University Press, 1925–47, 8 vols. in progress, see Vols. I–VII); Thomas Middleton, *Michaelmas Term, The Roaring Girl, A Trick to catch the old one*, see *Plays* (Editor, A. H. Bullen, Nimmo, 1885–6, 8 vols.); Philip Massinger, *A New Way to pay Old Debts, The City Madam*, see *Best Plays* (Editor, A. Symons, Mermaid Series: Benn, 2 vols., 1904, etc.).

[22] John Dryden, *Essay of Dramatic Poetry*, 1668, quoted by Knights (*op. cit.*, pp. 294–6).

[23] J. L. Palmer, *The Comedy of Manners* (Bell, 1913, p. 91), puts the matter in a nut-shell: "there was form and there was bad form. The whole duty of man was to find the one and eschew the other." For the work of Brome as an anticipation of later developments, see Kathleen M. Lynch, *The Social Mode of Restoration Comedy* (University of Michigan, New York, 1926, p. 34).

[24] See, e.g., the titles of some university chairs of natural science. When Keats wrote à propos of the rainbow "Philosophy will clip an angel's wings" and Wordsworth described a "philosopher" as "one who will peep and botanize upon his mother's grave", it was not to metaphysicians that the poets were referring.

# BIBLIOGRAPHICAL NOTE

The reader who enjoys the contemporary flavour may consult, in addition to the works of the dramatists:

(1) J. Dover Wilson, *Life in Shakespeare's England* (see p. 38, *note* 15), which contains well-chosen extracts from contemporary writings illustrating different aspects of Elizabethan life.

(2) Lothrop Withington, *Elizabethan England* (see p. 37, *note* 8), consisting of passages from William Harrison's *Description of Britain* with a characteristic introduction by F. J. Furnivall. Harrison is a charming and amusing writer.

(3) R. H. Tawney and Eileen Power, *Tudor Economic Documents* (Longmans, Green, 1924, 3 vols., see Vol. III), which also contain selections from contemporary works.

(4) The secondary books are innumerable, but the following may be mentioned:

L. C. Knights, *Drama and Society in the Age of Jonson* (Chatto & Windus, 1937). A study of social changes under Elizabeth and the first two Stuarts, and of the reflection of them in the works of the dramatists.

J. B. Black, *The Reign of Elizabeth, 1558–1603* (Oxford University Press, 1936). Contains two valuable, if necessarily somewhat summary, chapters (VII and VIII) on "The Expansion of England and the Economic and Social Revolution" and "Literature, Art and Thought".

G. M. Trevelyan, *England under the Stuarts* (Methuen, 1904). The first chapter paints a vivid and attractive picture of English social life under James I.

G. M. Trevelyan, *English Social History: a survey of six centuries, Chaucer to Queen Victoria* (Longmans, Green, 1944). Contains instructive chapters on the England of Elizabeth and the early Stuarts.

*Shakespeare's England* (Oxford University Press, 1916, 2 vols.). Contains chapters by well-known authorities on different sides of Elizabethan life.

E. K. Chambers, *The Elizabethan Stage* (Oxford University Press 1923, 4 vols.). The classical work on the drama.

*The Cambridge History of English Literature* (Editors, A. W. Ward and A. R. Waller, Cambridge University Press, 1907–16. Index volume, 1927. 15 vols.). The relevant volumes should be consulted.

A. Harbage, *Shakespeare's Audience* (Columbia University Press, New York: Oxford University Press, London, 1941).